POLICIES AND PROCEDURES IN ASSOCIATION MANAGEMENT: A BENCHMARKING GUIDE

Volume 4

Financial Operations
Office Management

Published by ASAE & The Center for Association Leadership
Washington, DC

Research, Editorial, and Production Staff

Project Management: Monica Dignam
Director, Industry & Market Research Department

Haisong Peng
Research Associate, Industry & Market Research Department

Implementation: Shawn E. Six
Partner, Industry Insights, Inc., Columbus, Ohio

Production: Baron Williams, Director, ASAE Book Publishing

This book is available at a special discount when ordered in bulk quantities. For information, contact the Member Service Center toll free at (888) 950-ASAE.

A complete catalog of titles is available on the ASAE Web site at www.asaenet.org/bookstore.

American Society of Association Executives
1575 I Street, N.W.
Washington, D.C. 20005-1103
(202) 626-2723

Cover design by Beth Lower, Director, Art
International Standard Book Number: 0-88034-265-X
Printed in the United States of America

10 9 8 7 6 5 4 3 2 1

Table of Contents

Acknowledgements

This edition of the *Policies and Procedures in Association Management: A Benchmarking Guide* (P & P) was truly a collaborative effort. Because of the depth and breadth of this study, input in almost every area of association management was required from association executives and other staff. The ASAE & The Center for Association Leadership volunteer leadership provided such input. We are grateful for their suggestions and contributions that helped to make this publication a useful benchmarking tool. We are also thankful to the many staff that offered recommendations for improving the study.

Our deepest appreciation is extended to the association executives and other staff who took the time to complete the survey. Thank you for sharing the policies and procedures of your organization with the rest of the association community.

Comments about this study are welcome, and feedback about improvements for future editions can be directed to research@asaenet.org.

Using This Publication

Executives look to the P & P to guide them with critical decisions that impact their organizations. In some cases, they need objective data to provide confirmation of (or peace of mind about) their decisions. Executives also rely on the P & P prior to restructuring departments or launching groundbreaking programs and services. In addition, the P & P has served as a must-read manual for those entrepreneurs in the formative stages of developing an association.

Other decision makers such as boards of directors, officers, and volunteer committees use P & P for guidance as they compare their organizations' practices with their peers. The P & P also has served as a resource for for-profit companies that hope to understand more about association operations as they seek to serve the association marketplace. These include businesses such as association management companies (AMCs), management consulting firms, public relations agencies, human resource consultants, and other aspiring businesses and entrepreneurs.

These and other for-profit executives use this publication to gauge the latest trends among associations and other nonprofit organizations so that they can strategize accordingly.

Seven-Volume Publication: In an effort to make the publication affordable for all potential users and more specific to their need for data by functional area, this edition of P & P is organized in seven separate volumes. The *Introduction & Organization Profile* is complimentary to anyone who purchases one or more of the seven companion volumes.

Users have the option of purchasing any combination of volumes that suit their needs. For example, a director of membership development may frequently consult Volume 1, which contains information on membership services and dues. This individual may also require the data on marketing and public relations in Volume 6. The table on the following page shows the topics covered in each volume.

Index to Functional Areas by Volume

	Base Volume	Volume 1	Volume 2	Volume 3	Volume 4	Volume 5	Volume 6	Volume 7
Organizational Structure & Profile	X							
Advertising							X	
Certification, Accreditation, Licensing, & Standards								X
Communications							X	
Components: Chapters & Other Communities						X		
Conventions & Meetings								X
Diversity				X				
Education & Professional Development								X
Financial Operations					X			
Government Affairs						X		
Governance Issues						X		
Human Resources				X				
Legal Issues						X		
Marketing							X	
Membership		X						
Office Management					X			
Publications							X	
Public Relations							X	
Research							X	
Technology			X					

To purchase additional volumes, please contact the member service center at 888-950-ASAE (2723) or visit our online bookstore at www.asaenet.org.

FINANCIAL OPERATIONS

Summary of Major Findings

Structure: 501(c)(6) organizations make up 56 percent of all respondents. More trade associations than individual membership organizations (IMOs) report this structure (66 percent vs. 47 percent respectively). 501(c)(3) organizations make up 37 percent of all responding organizations, more likely among IMOs than trade associations (46 percent vs. 26 percent respectively).

Staffing: Most organizations, 62 percent, report at least one full-time equivalent (FTE) with responsibility for financial operations. This position is equally likely by organization type but much more likely among organizations with more than ten FTEs. 61 percent report that staff with responsibility for this function is bonded.

One in three respondents, 36 percent, report that their organization's financial system includes a business continuity plan.

Outsourcing: Except for audits, few financial operations functions are outsourced. Three-quarters of all respondents (74 percent) report that their organization outsources audits.

Budget, Expenses, and Reserves: Median annual budget is $1.9 million ranging from $267,500 in 1-2 FTE organizations to $27 million in organizations with 100 or more FTEs.

Median overhead is estimated at 13 percent. Regardless of the type of organization or number of FTEs, median overhead ranges from 12 percent to 15 percent.

Median liquid reserves (cash and cash equivalents) are 26 percent. Median liquid reserves are inversely related to the number of FTEs. As the number of FTEs increases, the median percentage of operating budget to liquid reserves decreases.

Total reserves to operating budget are a median of 50 percent. Median total reserves to operating budget range from a low of 42 percent in organizations with 3-5 FTEs to a high of 56 percent in organizations with 100 or more FTEs.

For most organizations the fiscal year begins with the calendar year (56 percent). The fewer the FTEs the more likely the fiscal year starts in January. If the fiscal year starts in any other month, the most likely month is July. Organizations with 30 or more FTEs are more likely than others to begin their fiscal year in July.

Investments, Capital Expenditures, and Borrowing: Some 70 percent of all respondents report that their organization has a formal investment policy. If they do, equities, federally insured CDs, and U.S. Treasuries are most frequently allowed.

Most organizations use the services of an outside investment counselor (78 percent). IMOs are more likely than trade associations to use an outside investment counselor (83 percent vs. 71 percent respectively).

Some 43 percent of all respondents report that their organization borrows money and of them 19 percent report that the organization has a debt policy.

Accounts Payable/Accounts Receivable: 40 percent of all respondents report that a volunteer officer's signature is required for checks over a median of $3,000. Requiring a volunteer officer's signature is inversely related to size by the number of FTEs. As organizations get larger, they are less likely to require a volunteer officer's signature.

One in four organizations use a lockbox (28 percent). Use of a lockbox increases as the number of FTEs increases. Of those who report the use of a lockbox, 88 percent use a domestic lockbox.

Some 71 percent of all organizations accept payment online. Accepting payment online is one of the few areas in financial operations where a significant change has taken place since the 2001 P & P. In 2001 just 39 percent of organizations reported accepting payment online. Significant increases in this practice are found regardless of organization type or number of FTEs.

Few organizations maintain accounts outside the United States (8 percent) although when organizations reach 30 or more staff this percentage increases to 20 percent.

Sponsored Services: Contracts for sponsored services are reported by 40 percent of respondents. Among organizations reporting sponsored service contracts 58 percent report treating all or some of the income derived as unrelated business taxable income (UBIT).

Publications: Most organizations, 79 percent, publish a flagship periodically issued publication. Of those that do, 78 percent report that it contains advertising and 39 percent of them pay UBIT on this income.

Reporting: Virtually all organizations report providing interim financial statements to their leadership. Most, 53 percent, provide these reports more than four times per year. Three quarters also provide members with an annual report or financial statement.

Audit/IRS/Tax: Most organizations, 87 percent, report that their organization's financial records are subject to an annual independent audit. Few (5 percent) report having been audited by the IRS in the last three years.

Trade associations are more likely than IMOs to report that their organizations is subject to the lobbying tax deductibility law of 1993 (49 percent vs. 30 percent respectively). If they are subject to the law, few have reduced their lobbying activities as a result. If they are subject to the tax, most organizations, 80 percent, notify members of the portion of their dues that is nondeductible. Median percent of non-deductible dues is estimated at 11 percent. If the organization is not subject to the tax, 4 percent reports paying the proxy tax.

Sarbanes Oxley (SO): Respondents were asked about Whistleblower policies, audit committees, and staff ethics statements. In all cases, responses are similar regardless of organization type with increasing probability of having the item in place as staff size increases.

Whistleblower Policy:
- 22 percent have
- 74 percent adopted after SO

Audit Committee:
- 52 percent have
- 24 percent in place after SO

Staff Ethics Statement:
- 48 percent have
- 18 percent adopted after SO

Financial Staff Ethics Statement
- 24 percent have
- 19 percent adopted after SO

Vendors: 29 percent of all respondents report that their organization has formal guidelines for evaluating and selecting vendors and 46 percent report that multiple vendor bids are required when purchasing supplies and services. If multiple bids are required 81 percent require multiple bids for purchases over a median of $5,000. Most report that the chief staff executive has the authority to make the final decision regarding the selection of vendors.

Healthcare Organizations

All questions in the P & P were cross-tabulated by whether or not the responding organization's primary interest/subject area is in healthcare. The following tables show the statistically significant differences between healthcare and all other types of organization on data covered in this volume. If not shown below, responses received from healthcare organizations were similar to responses received by all other types of organization.

Are Financial Management Staff Bonded?			
		Organization Type	
Volume 4 Table 3	Total	Healthcare	All Other
Number of Respondents	734	112	622
Yes	61%	72%	59%
No	39%	28%	41%

Does Organization Use a Lockbox?			
		Organization Type	
Volume 4 Table 22a	Total	Healthcare	All Other
Number of Respondents	754	116	638
Yes	28%	43%	26%
No	72%	57%	74%

Does Organization Accept Payment Online?			
		Organization Type	
Volume 4 Table 23a	Total	Healthcare	All Other
Number of Respondents	754	116	638
Yes	71%	81%	69%
No	29%	19%	31%

If Organization Subject to Lobbying Tax Deductibility Law, Does It Notify Members of the Portion of Non-Deductible Dues?			
		Organization Type	
Volume 4 Table 31c	Total	Healthcare	All Other
Number of Respondents	261	43	218
Yes	80%	91%	79%
No	20%	9%	21%

If Organization Has a Whistleblower Policy, Was That Policy Adopted Before or After Sarbanes Oxley?			
		Organization Type	
Volume 4 Table 32b	Total	Healthcare	All Other
Number of Respondents	188	33	155
Before	26%	15%	28%
After	74%	85%	72%

Does Organization Have Formal Guidelines for Evaluating and Selecting Vendors?			
		Organization Type	
Volume 4 Table 36	Total	Healthcare	All Other
Number of Respondents	746	115	631
Yes	29%	34%	28%
No	71%	66%	72%

Does Organization Require Multiple Vendor Bids ?			
		Organization Type	
Volume 4 Table 37a	Total	Healthcare	All Other
Number of Respondents	749	116	633
Yes	46%	56%	44%
No	54%	44%	56%

Index to Tables

Financial Operations

Table Number

Tax Status

Table 1
What is the primary IRS tax status of your organization (the primary or parent organization)?

		Organization Type		Number of FTEs					
	Total	Trade	IMO	2 or less	3-5	6-10	11-29	30-99	100 +
Number of Respondents	1,095	504	585	149	210	191	269	198	78
501 (c)(6)	56%	66%	47%	62%	62%	63%	51%	49%	42%
501 (c)(3)	37%	26%	46%	32%	31%	33%	41%	40%	47%
501 (c)(4)	2%	3%	2%	1%	2%	2%	4%	2%	4%
Not tax-exempt	2%	3%	2%	1%	3%	3%	2%	4%	1%
Other	3%	2%	3%	3%	1%	0%	3%	5%	5%

Staffing

Table 2
Percent of organizations reporting at least 1 FTE in Financial Operations:

		Organization Type		Number of FTEs					
	Total	Trade	IMO	2 or less	3-5	6-10	11-29	30-99	100 +
Number of Respondents	1,004	459	539	142	180	168	246	192	76
At least 1 FTE in Financial Operations	62%	62%	62%	2%	29%	58%	90%	96%	87%

Table 3
Are the members of your organization's financial management staff bonded?

		Organization Type		Number of FTEs					
	Total	Trade	IMO	2 or less	3-5	6-10	11-29	30-99	100 +
Number of Respondents	734	326	404	100	158	130	180	124	42
Yes	61%	60%	62%	49%	51%	60%	67%	69%	71%
No	39%	40%	38%	51%	49%	40%	33%	31%	29%

ф Percentages add to more than 100% due to multiple responses.
*Too few responses to obtain statistically valid information.
**Mean can be distorted due to very extreme values.
Note: Percentages may add to more or less than 100% due to rounding.

Table 4
Does your organization's financial system have a business continuity plan?

	Total	Organization Type		Number of FTEs					
		Trade	IMO	2 or less	3-5	6-10	11-29	30-99	100 +
Number of Respondents	727	322	401	99	158	126	180	121	43
Yes	36%	36%	35%	16%	23%	31%	37%	55%	79%
No	64%	64%	65%	84%	77%	69%	63%	45%	21%

Outsourcing

Table 5
Does your organization outsource any of the following functions? ⌖

	Total	Organization Type		Number of FTEs					
		Trade	IMO	2 or less	3-5	6-10	11-29	30-99	100 +
Number of Respondents	761	338	418	103	164	134	190	126	44
Accounts Payable (A/P)	12%	11%	14%	17%	18%	18%	6%	4%	14%
Accounts Receivable (A/R)	8%	9%	8%	14%	9%	15%	3%	4%	9%
Audits	74%	73%	75%	59%	70%	80%	80%	79%	68%
Cash control/treasury management	8%	8%	8%	12%	9%	8%	4%	4%	18%
Financial reporting	19%	16%	21%	29%	35%	18%	9%	6%	9%
Lockbox	21%	17%	25%	6%	5%	14%	24%	45%	57%
Risk management	7%	7%	7%	2%	9%	5%	4%	11%	11%
Tax or tax management	57%	55%	59%	57%	65%	58%	58%	50%	39%

⌖ Percentages add to more than 100% due to multiple responses.
*Too few responses to obtain statistically valid information.
**Mean can be distorted due to very extreme values.
Note: Percentages may add to more or less than 100% due to rounding.

Budget, Expenses and Reserves

Table 6a
Which of the following includes the range of your organization's budget?

		Organization Type		Number of FTEs					
	Total	Trade	IMO	2 or less	3-5	6-10	11-29	30-99	100 +
Number of Respondents	1,111	510	595	150	214	194	272	203	78
Less than $500,000	16%	15%	17%	81%	26%	2%	1%	0%	0%
$500,000 - $999,999	14%	14%	14%	14%	42%	21%	1%	<1%	0%
$1,000,000 - $1,999,999	18%	21%	15%	2%	24%	49%	17%	1%	0%
$2,000,000 - $4,999,999	20%	21%	20%	1%	6%	25%	53%	9%	1%
$5,000,000 - $9,999,999	14%	15%	13%	0%	1%	1%	25%	39%	1%
$10,000,000 - $14,999,999	6%	5%	7%	0%	<1%	0%	2%	26%	9%
$15,000,000 - $19,999,999	3%	3%	3%	0%	0%	0%	<1%	10%	13%
$20,000,000 - $49,999,999	5%	4%	7%	1%	0%	1%	1%	13%	37%
$50,000,000 - $74,999,999	1%	1%	2%	1%	0%	0%	0%	<1%	17%
$75,000,000 or more	2%	1%	3%	1%	<1%	2%	0%	<1%	22%

Table 6b
What is your organization's annual budget?

		Organization Type		Number of FTEs					
	Total	Trade	IMO	2 or less	3-5	6-10	11-29	30-99	100 +
Number of Respondents	740	329	406	100	158	131	185	123	43
Mean**	$6,437,123	$4,328,256	$8,170,083	$705,241	$1,026,247	$1,609,794	$4,113,872	$12,542,496	$46,886,596
Median	$1,900,000	$1,700,000	$2,097,025	$267,500	$800,000	$1,292,000	$3,065,000	$10,000,000	$27,000,000
25th Percentile	$750,000	$750,000	$750,000	$178,350	$463,000	$1,000,000	$2,300,000	$6,500,000	$18,000,000
75th Percentile	$5,500,000	$4,954,153	$6,500,000	$400,000	$1,050,000	$2,000,000	$5,000,000	$16,000,000	$52,000,000

Table 7
What percent of your annual expenses are classified as overhead expenses (e.g., utilities, building expense, etc.)?

		Organization Type		Number of FTEs					
	Total	Trade	IMO	2 or less	3-5	6-10	11-29	30-99	100 +
Number of Respondents	643	283	355	85	136	116	158	108	40
Mean**	16%	16%	15%	17%	18%	17%	15%	14%	14%
Median	13%	13%	13%	12%	15%	15%	13%	12%	12%
25th Percentile	7%	8%	6%	5%	9%	8%	7%	7%	6%
75th Percentile	20%	22%	20%	25%	25%	22%	20%	18%	20%

♦ Percentages add to more than 100% due to multiple responses.
*Too few responses to obtain statistically valid information.
**Mean can be distorted due to very extreme values.
Note: Percentages may add to more or less than 100% due to rounding.

Table 8
What percentage of your annual operating budget does your organization maintain in Liquid Reserves (e.g., cash and cash equivalents)?

	Total	Organization Type		Number of FTEs					
		Trade	IMO	2 or less	3-5	6-10	11-29	30-99	100 +
Number of Respondents	605	269	331	80	131	106	147	103	38
Mean**	40%	39%	39%	52%	45%	43%	35%	31%	27%
Median	26%	28%	25%	44%	30%	33%	25%	20%	25%
25th Percentile	12%	15%	10%	20%	15%	19%	12%	10%	9%
75th Percentile	53%	53%	50%	94%	75%	60%	45%	44%	40%

Table 9
What percentage of your annual operating budget does your organization aim to maintain in Liquid Reserves (e.g., cash and cash equivalents)?

	Total	Organization Type		Number of FTEs					
		Trade	IMO	2 or less	3-5	6-10	11-29	30-99	100 +
Number of Respondents	517	231	281	68	110	93	126	89	31
Mean**	40%	39%	40%	57%	43%	42%	35%	33%	27%
Median	30%	32%	25%	50%	35%	45%	25%	20%	20%
25th Percentile	15%	15%	12%	20%	17%	20%	15%	10%	10%
75th Percentile	50%	50%	50%	100%	60%	50%	50%	41%	50%

Table 10
What percentage of your annual operating budget does your organization maintain in Total Reserves (e.g., Net Assets)?

	Total	Organization Type		Number of FTEs					
		Trade	IMO	2 or less	3-5	6-10	11-29	30-99	100 +
Number of Respondents	547	236	307	62	111	90	141	103	40
Mean**	61%	56%	65%	53%	53%	73%	56%	68%	69%
Median	50%	50%	50%	50%	42%	52%	48%	50%	56%
25th Percentile	28%	25%	29%	25%	21%	30%	25%	31%	41%
75th Percentile	80%	77%	90%	75%	75%	95%	79%	80%	98%

✟ Percentages add to more than 100% due to multiple responses.
*Too few responses to obtain statistically valid information.
**Mean can be distorted due to very extreme values.
Note: Percentages may add to more or less than 100% due to rounding.

Table 11
What percentage of your annual operating budget does your organization aim to maintain in Total Reserves (e.g., Net Assets)?

		Organization Type		Number of FTEs					
	Total	Trade	IMO	2 or less	3-5	6-10	11-29	30-99	100 +
Number of Respondents	487	212	271	53	103	82	123	92	34
Mean**	68%	64%	73%	63%	64%	78%	66%	73%	66%
Median	50%	50%	50%	50%	50%	60%	50%	50%	50%
25th Percentile	40%	34%	40%	24%	30%	50%	40%	45%	40%
75th Percentile	100%	100%	100%	75%	91%	100%	90%	100%	100%

Table 12
In what month does your organization's fiscal year begin?

		Organization Type		Number of FTEs					
	Total	Trade	IMO	2 or less	3-5	6-10	11-29	30-99	100 +
Number of Respondents	739	325	409	102	159	132	180	124	42
January	56%	61%	53%	68%	58%	49%	57%	56%	43%
February	1%	1%	0%	0%	1%	0%	1%	1%	0%
March	<1%	1%	<1%	0%	1%	1%	1%	0%	0%
April	4%	3%	4%	3%	3%	3%	5%	3%	2%
May	2%	3%	2%	3%	1%	3%	3%	2%	2%
June	3%	2%	3%	5%	1%	3%	2%	3%	5%
July	18%	14%	21%	11%	18%	17%	17%	22%	31%
August	2%	1%	2%	3%	1%	2%	1%	2%	2%
September	3%	2%	4%	3%	3%	3%	3%	4%	5%
October	8%	7%	9%	1%	11%	13%	6%	7%	10%
November	2%	2%	1%	1%	1%	2%	3%	1%	0%
December	2%	3%	1%	3%	1%	3%	2%	0%	0%

Table 13
What method of accounting does your organization use?

		Organization Type		Number of FTEs					
	Total	Trade	IMO	2 or less	3-5	6-10	11-29	30-99	100 +
Number of Respondents	742	331	407	102	159	130	183	124	44
Accrual	64%	63%	65%	41%	45%	63%	73%	86%	91%
Cash	19%	19%	19%	45%	35%	18%	9%	2%	2%
Combination	15%	16%	14%	12%	19%	17%	17%	10%	5%
Don't know	1%	2%	1%	2%	1%	2%	1%	2%	2%

ᵠ Percentages add to more than 100% due to multiple responses.
*Too few responses to obtain statistically valid information.
**Mean can be distorted due to very extreme values.
Note: Percentages may add to more or less than 100% due to rounding.

Table 14
Who has final authority over the budget?

	Total	Organization Type		Number of FTEs					
		Trade	IMO	2 or less	3-5	6-10	11-29	30-99	100 +
Number of Respondents	754	336	413	103	161	134	189	123	44
Chief staff executive	16%	18%	15%	8%	17%	14%	19%	24%	7%
Controller/CFO	1%	1%	1%	1%	1%	1%	1%	1%	2%
Department Head	<1%	0%	<1%	0%	0%	0%	0%	1%	0%
Finance or other committee	3%	3%	4%	2%	4%	2%	3%	7%	2%
Board of Directors	77%	76%	77%	85%	75%	82%	75%	67%	80%
Other	3%	2%	3%	4%	2%	1%	3%	1%	9%

Investments, Capital Expenditures and Borrowing

Table 15a
Does your organization have a formal investment policy for organization funds?

	Total	Organization Type		Number of FTEs					
		Trade	IMO	2 or less	3-5	6-10	11-29	30-99	100 +
Number of Respondents	757	335	417	103	163	133	188	126	44
Yes	70%	67%	72%	29%	62%	69%	81%	89%	95%
No	30%	33%	28%	71%	38%	31%	19%	11%	5%

Table 15b
If yes, what types of investments are allowed in the portfolio? ⌖

	Total	Organization Type		Number of FTEs					
		Trade	IMO	2 or less	3-5	6-10	11-29	30-99	100 +
Number of Respondents	530	226	301	30	101	92	153	112	42
Alternative investments (REITs, hedge funds, private equities)	9%	7%	11%	0%	5%	13%	5%	12%	24%
Corporate bonds	48%	45%	51%	20%	33%	46%	52%	62%	67%
Equities	55%	47%	60%	30%	35%	49%	61%	70%	71%
Federally insured CDs	52%	58%	49%	53%	59%	60%	54%	46%	29%
International investments/securities	24%	19%	28%	7%	12%	21%	24%	34%	48%
U.S. Treasuries	51%	53%	50%	33%	44%	47%	56%	58%	57%
Other	22%	20%	23%	33%	21%	26%	19%	19%	24%

⌖ Percentages add to more than 100% due to multiple responses.
*Too few responses to obtain statistically valid information.
**Mean can be distorted due to very extreme values.
Note: Percentages may add to more or less than 100% due to rounding.

Table 15c
If yes, what percentage of the portfolio does each of the investments comprise (average)?

		Organization Type		Number of FTEs					
	Total	Trade	IMO	2 or less	3-5	6-10	11-29	30-99	100 +
Number of Respondents	422	177	242	24	72	75	117	94	40
Alternative investment (REITs, hedge funds, private equities)	2%	1%	2%	0%	0%	3%	1%	2%	3%
Corporate bonds	16%	16%	15%	5%	14%	14%	14%	20%	24%
Equities	31%	24%	36%	22%	20%	28%	31%	38%	43%
Federally-insured CD	23%	29%	19%	48%	33%	27%	26%	11%	3%
International investments/securities	4%	3%	4%	1%	2%	4%	4%	4%	6%
U.S. Treasuries	13%	15%	12%	4%	11%	13%	14%	16%	16%
Other	12%	12%	12%	20%	20%	11%	10%	9%	6%

Table 16
Does your organization use the services of an outside investment counselor?

		Organization Type		Number of FTEs					
	Total	Trade	IMO	2 or less	3-5	6-10	11-29	30-99	100 +
Number of Respondents	518	223	292	30	98	91	149	109	41
Yes	78%	71%	83%	50%	65%	76%	81%	87%	95%
No	22%	29%	17%	50%	35%	24%	19%	13%	5%

Table 17
Who sets investing strategy in your organization? ⌖

		Organization Type		Number of FTEs					
	Total	Trade	IMO	2 or less	3-5	6-10	11-29	30-99	100 +
Number of Respondents	761	338	418	103	164	134	190	126	44
Chief staff executive	35%	36%	34%	30%	40%	40%	36%	29%	25%
Controller/CFO	18%	19%	18%	5%	5%	10%	29%	32%	41%
Department Head	1%	1%	1%	0%	0%	0%	1%	2%	2%
Deputy staff executive	1%	<1%	2%	0%	1%	1%	2%	2%	0%
Finance or other committee	52%	49%	55%	35%	45%	52%	52%	67%	68%
Board of Directors	56%	54%	57%	61%	57%	60%	56%	44%	57%
Other	6%	5%	7%	3%	10%	5%	6%	5%	5%

⌖ Percentages add to more than 100% due to multiple responses.
*Too few responses to obtain statistically valid information.
**Mean can be distorted due to very extreme values.
Note: Percentages may add to more or less than 100% due to rounding.

Table 18

Who has the day-to-day authority to invest organization funds? ⌖

		Organization Type		Number of FTEs					
	Total	Trade	IMO	2 or less	3-5	6-10	11-29	30-99	100 +
Number of Respondents	761	338	418	103	164	134	190	126	44
Chief staff executive	55%	55%	55%	51%	65%	65%	57%	41%	27%
Controller/CFO	36%	37%	35%	6%	10%	19%	54%	70%	80%
Department Head	1%	1%	1%	1%	0%	0%	1%	4%	0%
Deputy staff executive	3%	1%	4%	0%	0%	1%	4%	9%	5%
Finance or other committee	16%	14%	19%	21%	18%	23%	15%	7%	11%
Board of Directors	14%	14%	13%	33%	20%	16%	7%	2%	2%
Other	9%	7%	10%	10%	8%	9%	6%	13%	9%

Table 19

Does your organization have a capital expenditures policy?

		Organization Type		Number of FTEs					
	Total	Trade	IMO	2 or less	3-5	6-10	11-29	30-99	100 +
Number of Respondents	748	333	410	102	159	133	187	124	43
Yes	40%	37%	44%	15%	22%	32%	49%	69%	77%
No	60%	63%	56%	85%	78%	68%	51%	31%	23%

Table 20a

Does your organization borrow money?

		Organization Type		Number of FTEs					
	Total	Trade	IMO	2 or less	3-5	6-10	11-29	30-99	100 +
Number of Respondents	752	335	413	102	161	133	189	124	43
Yes	43%	45%	42%	29%	36%	47%	48%	48%	58%
No	57%	55%	58%	71%	64%	53%	52%	52%	42%

⌖ Percentages add to more than 100% due to multiple responses.

*Too few responses to obtain statistically valid information.

**Mean can be distorted due to very extreme values.

Note: Percentages may add to more or less than 100% due to rounding.

Table 20b
If yes, does your organization have a debt policy?

	Total	Organization Type		Number of FTEs					
		Trade	IMO	2 or less	3-5	6-10	11-29	30-99	100 +
Number of Respondents	318	147	170	29	57	60	89	58	25
Yes	19%	12%	25%	17%	16%	20%	15%	24%	32%
No	81%	88%	75%	83%	84%	80%	85%	76%	68%

Accounts Payable/Accounts Receivable

Table 21a
Does your organization require a countersignature by a volunteer officer on checks over a certain amount?

	Total	Organization Type		Number of FTEs					
		Trade	IMO	2 or less	3-5	6-10	11-29	30-99	100 +
Number of Respondents	754	336	413	103	162	134	189	124	42
Yes	40%	39%	41%	60%	52%	49%	32%	20%	19%
No	60%	61%	59%	40%	48%	51%	68%	80%	81%

Table 21b
If yes, what amount?

	Total	Organization Type		Number of FTEs					
		Trade	IMO	2 or less	3-5	6-10	11-29	30-99	100 +
Number of Respondents	279	121	155	57	75	60	59	22	6
Mean**	$7,890	$6,807	$8,694	$2,590	$5,811	$6,033	$14,725	$10,273	$26,833
Median	$3,000	$2,500	$3,500	$1,000	$5,000	$5,000	$5,000	$3,750	$15,000
25th Percentile	$500	$500	$1,000	$1	$500	$500	$2,000	$1,000	$5,000
75th Percentile	$10,000	$8,125	$10,000	$4,250	$6,000	$9,000	$15,000	$10,000	$25,000

Table 22a
Does your organization use a lockbox?

	Total	Organization Type		Number of FTEs					
		Trade	IMO	2 or less	3-5	6-10	11-29	30-99	100 +
Number of Respondents	754	334	415	103	162	131	189	125	44
Yes	28%	20%	34%	9%	11%	20%	29%	56%	75%
No	72%	80%	66%	91%	89%	80%	71%	44%	25%

⧫ Percentages add to more than 100% due to multiple responses.
*Too few responses to obtain statistically valid information.
**Mean can be distorted due to very extreme values.
Note: Percentages may add to more or less than 100% due to rounding.

Table 22b
If yes, is the lockbox. . .

	Total	Organization Type		Number of FTEs					
		Trade	IMO	2 or less	3-5	6-10	11-29	30-99	100 +
Number of Respondents	208	67	140	9	17	26	53	70	33
Domestic	88%	88%	87%	78%	100%	85%	85%	89%	88%
International	0%	0%	0%	0%	0%	0%	0%	0%	0%
Both	13%	12%	13%	22%	0%	15%	15%	11%	12%

Table 22c
If yes, why does your organization use a lockbox? ᶲ

	Total	Organization Type		Number of FTEs					
		Trade	IMO	2 or less	3-5	6-10	11-29	30-99	100 +
Number of Respondents	210	67	142	9	18	26	54	70	33
Accounting controls offered	66%	72%	63%	22%	22%	65%	70%	74%	76%
Transaction volume	56%	51%	58%	22%	17%	35%	63%	66%	70%
Speed of deposit of funds	72%	73%	71%	22%	22%	69%	74%	84%	85%
Other	9%	9%	8%	11%	28%	8%	7%	4%	9%

Table 23a
Does your organization accept payment online?

	Total	Organization Type		Number of FTEs					
		Trade	IMO	2 or less	3-5	6-10	11-29	30-99	100 +
Number of Respondents	754	334	415	103	161	133	188	125	44
Yes	71%	60%	81%	43%	60%	71%	82%	87%	91%
No	29%	40%	19%	57%	40%	29%	18%	13%	9%

Table 23b
If yes, in what form are online payments accepted?

	Total	Organization Type		Number of FTEs					
		Trade	IMO	2 or less	3-5	6-10	11-29	30-99	100 +
Number of Respondents	539	201	335	44	97	95	154	109	40
ACH (automated clearinghouse)	2%	2%	1%	2%	0%	3%	3%	1%	0%
Credit card	76%	76%	77%	80%	84%	79%	75%	72%	68%
Both ACH and credit card	21%	21%	21%	16%	15%	17%	22%	27%	33%

ᶲ Percentages add to more than 100% due to multiple responses.
*Too few responses to obtain statistically valid information.
**Mean can be distorted due to very extreme values.
Note: Percentages may add to more or less than 100% due to rounding.

Table 24a
Does your organization maintain accounts outside the United States?

	Total	Organization Type		Number of FTEs					
		Trade	IMO	2 or less	3-5	6-10	11-29	30-99	100 +
Number of Respondents	753	335	413	102	162	134	187	125	43
Yes	8%	7%	8%	1%	4%	1%	7%	20%	23%
No	92%	93%	92%	99%	96%	99%	93%	80%	77%

Table 24b
If yes, why does your organization maintain accounts outside the United States? ⴲ

	Total	Organization Type		Number of FTEs					
		Trade	IMO	2 or less	3-5	6-10	11-29	30-99	100 +
Number of Respondents	58	23	35	1	7	2	13	25	10
Component support (chapters, branches, etc.)	38%	30%	43%	0%	43%	0%	23%	36%	70%
Dues collection	34%	39%	31%	0%	57%	0%	31%	32%	40%
Exchange rate fluctuation protection	28%	26%	29%	0%	29%	0%	31%	24%	40%
Meetings expenses	36%	35%	37%	0%	57%	0%	23%	32%	60%
Payment for publications	10%	9%	11%	0%	0%	0%	0%	8%	40%
Other	33%	43%	26%	100%	43%	100%	15%	36%	20%

Sponsored Services

Table 25a
Does your organization have separate contract for sponsored services: e.g., a licensing agreement that allows the vendor to use the organization's name and logo to market the program while paying a royalty; and a services agreement whereby the vendor pays?

	Total	Organization Type		Number of FTEs					
		Trade	IMO	2 or less	3-5	6-10	11-29	30-99	100 +
Number of Respondents	537	247	288	64	106	101	135	92	39
Yes	40%	39%	41%	30%	23%	32%	50%	59%	51%
No	60%	61%	59%	70%	77%	68%	50%	41%	49%

ⴲ Percentages add to more than 100% due to multiple responses.
*Too few responses to obtain statistically valid information.
**Mean can be distorted due to very extreme values.
Note: Percentages may add to more or less than 100% due to rounding.

Table 25b
If yes, does your organization treat some or all income from sponsored services as unrelated business taxable income (UBIT)?

	Total	Organization Type		Number of FTEs					
		Trade	IMO	2 or less	3-5	6-10	11-29	30-99	100 +
Number of Respondents	204	93	111	19	20	31	65	50	19
Yes	58%	55%	60%	42%	40%	61%	55%	70%	63%
No	42%	45%	40%	58%	60%	39%	45%	30%	37%

Publications

Table 26a
Does your organization publish a flagship periodically issued publication?

	Total	Organization Type		Number of FTEs					
		Trade	IMO	2 or less	3-5	6-10	11-29	30-99	100 +
Number of Respondents	467	195	271	57	79	71	124	91	45
Yes	79%	72%	85%	60%	65%	75%	85%	91%	96%
No	21%	28%	15%	40%	35%	25%	15%	9%	4%

Table 26b
If yes, does it contain paid advertising?

	Total	Organization Type		Number of FTEs					
		Trade	IMO	2 or less	3-5	6-10	11-29	30-99	100 +
Number of Respondents	366	139	226	33	51	53	104	83	42
Yes	78%	74%	81%	73%	59%	77%	84%	82%	88%
No	22%	26%	19%	27%	41%	23%	16%	18%	12%

Table 26c
If paid advertising is accepted, does your organization pay any (net) unrelated business income tax (UBIT) on this advertising income?

	Total	Organization Type		Number of FTEs					
		Trade	IMO	2 or less	3-5	6-10	11-29	30-99	100 +
Number of Respondents	287	104	183	27	29	41	89	69	32
Yes	39%	37%	41%	19%	34%	34%	33%	51%	63%
No	61%	63%	59%	81%	66%	66%	67%	49%	38%

✦ Percentages add to more than 100% due to multiple responses.
*Too few responses to obtain statistically valid information.
**Mean can be distorted due to very extreme values.
Note: Percentages may add to more or less than 100% due to rounding.

Reporting

Table 27a
Does your organization provide interim financial statements to your leadership?

		Organization Type		Number of FTEs					
	Total	Trade	IMO	2 or less	3-5	6-10	11-29	30-99	100 +
Number of Respondents	754	336	413	103	162	133	188	124	44
Yes	96%	97%	96%	91%	97%	97%	98%	98%	93%
No	4%	3%	4%	9%	3%	3%	2%	2%	7%

Table 27b
If yes, how many times per year?

		Organization Type		Number of FTEs					
	Total	Trade	IMO	2 or less	3-5	6-10	11-29	30-99	100 +
Number of Respondents	696	318	374	91	152	123	176	116	38
One	1%	1%	1%	1%	1%	2%	2%	0%	0%
Two	4%	4%	3%	5%	6%	4%	3%	3%	0%
Three	7%	7%	8%	7%	5%	7%	9%	9%	13%
Four	34%	34%	34%	27%	39%	33%	32%	35%	34%
More than four	53%	53%	54%	59%	50%	54%	54%	53%	53%

Table 28
Does your organization provide an annual report or financial statement to members?

		Organization Type		Number of FTEs					
	Total	Trade	IMO	2 or less	3-5	6-10	11-29	30-99	100 +
Number of Respondents	749	333	411	102	160	134	188	122	43
Yes	77%	76%	79%	71%	73%	77%	80%	80%	95%
No	23%	24%	21%	29%	28%	23%	20%	20%	5%

† Percentages add to more than 100% due to multiple responses.
*Too few responses to obtain statistically valid information.
**Mean can be distorted due to very extreme values.
Note: Percentages may add to more or less than 100% due to rounding.

Audit/IRS/Tax

Table 29
Does an independent auditor audit your organization's financial records annually?

	Total	Organization Type		Number of FTEs					
		Trade	IMO	2 or less	3-5	6-10	11-29	30-99	100 +
Number of Respondents	752	335	412	102	162	133	188	123	44
Yes	87%	87%	87%	60%	77%	89%	97%	99%	100%
No	13%	13%	13%	40%	23%	11%	3%	1%	0%

Table 30a
Within the past 3 years, has your organization been audited by the IRS?

	Total	Organization Type		Number of FTEs					
		Trade	IMO	2 or less	3-5	6-10	11-29	30-99	100 +
Number of Respondents	755	337	413	103	162	134	189	123	44
Yes	5%	5%	4%	5%	4%	2%	7%	2%	11%
No	95%	95%	96%	95%	96%	98%	93%	98%	89%

ф Percentages add to more than 100% due to multiple responses.
*Too few responses to obtain statistically valid information.
**Mean can be distorted due to very extreme values.
Note: Percentages may add to more or less than 100% due to rounding.

Table 30b
If yes, what were the points at issue in the IRS audit? ⌖

	Total	Organization Type		Number of FTEs					
		Trade	IMO	2 or less	3-5	6-10	11-29	30-99	100 +
Number of Respondents	36	18	18	5	7	3	13	3	5
Corporate sponsorship income	0%	0%	0%	0%	0%	0%	0%	0%	0%
Employee vs. independent contractor	11%	11%	11%	20%	0%	0%	8%	0%	40%
For-profit subsidiary corporations	6%	6%	6%	20%	14%	0%	0%	0%	0%
Foundations or other tax-exempt subsidiaries	6%	6%	6%	0%	0%	0%	15%	0%	0%
Insurance sponsorship income	6%	0%	11%	0%	14%	0%	8%	0%	0%
Lobbying and/or political activity	17%	28%	6%	40%	14%	33%	15%	0%	0%
Mailing list rentals/affinity credit cards or other sponsorships or vendor products or services	0%	0%	0%	0%	0%	0%	0%	0%	0%
Periodical advertising income	11%	11%	11%	20%	14%	0%	8%	33%	0%
Reporting and disclosure requirements	0%	0%	0%	0%	0%	0%	0%	0%	0%
Retirement plans	14%	11%	17%	0%	0%	67%	8%	0%	40%
Supplier membership dues income	3%	6%	0%	0%	14%	0%	0%	0%	0%
Trade show income	0%	0%	0%	0%	0%	0%	0%	0%	0%
Unrelated business income tax (UBIT) issues not detailed above	14%	11%	17%	20%	14%	0%	15%	33%	0%
Not given	12%	10%	15%	0%	16%	0%	23%	33%	20%

Table 31a
Is your organization subject to the lobbying tax deductibility law of 1993?

	Total	Organization Type		Number of FTEs					
		Trade	IMO	2 or less	3-5	6-10	11-29	30-99	100 +
Number of Respondents	741	326	410	100	161	129	187	121	43
Yes	38%	49%	30%	28%	35%	33%	44%	43%	53%
No	62%	51%	70%	72%	65%	67%	56%	57%	47%

⌖ Percentages add to more than 100% due to multiple responses.
*Too few responses to obtain statistically valid information.
**Mean can be distorted due to very extreme values.
Note: Percentages may add to more or less than 100% due to rounding.

Table 31b
If yes, has the tax caused your organization to reduce its lobbying activities?

		Organization Type		Number of FTEs					
	Total	Trade	IMO	2 or less	3-5	6-10	11-29	30-99	100 +
Number of Respondents	262	149	112	25	52	41	76	47	21
Yes	4%	5%	4%	4%	6%	12%	0%	4%	0%
No	96%	95%	96%	96%	94%	88%	100%	96%	100%

Table 31c
If yes, does your organization notify members of the portion of their dues that is non-deductible?

		Organization Type		Number of FTEs					
	Total	Trade	IMO	2 or less	3-5	6-10	11-29	30-99	100 +
Number of Respondents	261	148	112	27	54	39	74	47	20
Yes	80%	80%	81%	67%	81%	87%	84%	70%	95%
No	20%	20%	19%	33%	19%	13%	16%	30%	5%

Table 31d
If organization notifies members, what is the non-deductible percentage?

		Organization Type		Number of FTEs					
	Total	Trade	IMO	2 or less	3-5	6-10	11-29	30-99	100 +
Number of Respondents	190	109	81	16	41	27	57	30	19
Mean	16%	19%	12%	19%	19%	12%	14%	19%	14%
Median	11%	15%	8%	11%	15%	10%	10%	11%	10%
25th Percentile	5%	9%	3%	7%	9%	5%	5%	5%	5%
75th Percentile	20%	24%	15%	18%	22%	19%	19%	26%	24%

Table 31e
If organization is not subject to tax, does your organization pay the proxy tax?

		Organization Type		Number of FTEs					
	Total	Trade	IMO	2 or less	3-5	6-10	11-29	30-99	100 +
Number of Respondents	223	77	143	35	49	40	49	39	11
Yes	4%	6%	3%	3%	8%	3%	0%	8%	0%
No	96%	94%	97%	97%	92%	98%	100%	92%	100%

⧫ Percentages add to more than 100% due to multiple responses.
*Too few responses to obtain statistically valid information.
**Mean can be distorted due to very extreme values.
Note: Percentages may add to more or less than 100% due to rounding.

Sarbanes Oxley

Table 32a
Has your organization adopted a Whistleblower Policy?

		Organization Type		Number of FTEs					
	Total	Trade	IMO	2 or less	3-5	6-10	11-29	30-99	100 +
Number of Respondents	869	390	475	116	176	151	221	150	55
Yes	22%	24%	21%	4%	8%	21%	24%	38%	64%
No	78%	76%	79%	96%	92%	79%	76%	62%	36%

Table 32b
If yes, did you adopt that policy before or after Sarbanes Oxley was enacted?

		Organization Type		Number of FTEs					
	Total	Trade	IMO	2 or less	3-5	6-10	11-29	30-99	100 +
Number of Respondents	188	89	98	5	14	31	50	54	34
Before Sarbanes Oxley	26%	25%	27%	0%	57%	19%	16%	33%	26%
After Sarbanes Oxley	74%	75%	73%	100%	43%	81%	84%	67%	74%

Table 33a
Does your organization have an Audit Committee?

		Organization Type		Number of FTEs					
	Total	Trade	IMO	2 or less	3-5	6-10	11-29	30-99	100 +
Number of Respondents	874	393	478	118	173	153	222	152	56
Yes	52%	51%	53%	30%	35%	48%	59%	71%	88%
No	48%	49%	47%	70%	65%	52%	41%	29%	13%

Table 33b
If yes, was that committee in place before or after Sarbanes Oxley was enacted?

		Organization Type		Number of FTEs					
	Total	Trade	IMO	2 or less	3-5	6-10	11-29	30-99	100 +
Number of Respondents	448	194	252	34	61	73	127	105	48
Before Sarbanes Oxley	76%	78%	74%	88%	84%	77%	70%	71%	81%
After Sarbanes Oxley	24%	22%	26%	12%	16%	23%	30%	29%	19%

⌖ Percentages add to more than 100% due to multiple responses.
*Too few responses to obtain statistically valid information.
**Mean can be distorted due to very extreme values.
Note: Percentages may add to more or less than 100% due to rounding.

Table 34a
Does your organization have a staff ethics statement?

	Total	Organization Type		Number of FTEs					
		Trade	IMO	2 or less	3-5	6-10	11-29	30-99	100 +
Number of Respondents	868	387	477	116	175	151	221	150	55
Yes	48%	46%	50%	22%	40%	46%	54%	63%	71%
No	52%	54%	50%	78%	60%	54%	46%	37%	29%

Table 34b
If yes, was that statement adopted before or after Sarbanes Oxley was enacted?

	Total	Organization Type		Number of FTEs					
		Trade	IMO	2 or less	3-5	6-10	11-29	30-99	100 +
Number of Respondents	401	168	231	23	65	68	115	91	39
Before Sarbanes Oxley	82%	79%	84%	78%	88%	78%	80%	82%	85%
After Sarbanes Oxley	18%	21%	16%	22%	12%	22%	20%	18%	15%

Table 35a
Does your organization have a financial staff ethics statement?

	Total	Organization Type		Number of FTEs					
		Trade	IMO	2 or less	3-5	6-10	11-29	30-99	100 +
Number of Respondents	864	389	471	117	175	151	221	146	54
Yes	24%	22%	26%	10%	24%	25%	24%	33%	31%
No	76%	78%	74%	90%	76%	75%	76%	67%	69%

Table 35b
If yes, was that statement adopted before or after Sarbanes Oxley was enacted?

	Total	Organization Type		Number of FTEs					
		Trade	IMO	2 or less	3-5	6-10	11-29	30-99	100 +
Number of Respondents	195	81	114	10	38	36	51	43	17
Before Sarbanes Oxley	81%	79%	82%	90%	84%	72%	84%	77%	82%
After Sarbanes Oxley	19%	21%	18%	10%	16%	28%	16%	23%	18%

⧫ Percentages add to more than 100% due to multiple responses.
*Too few responses to obtain statistically valid information.
**Mean can be distorted due to very extreme values.
Note: Percentages may add to more or less than 100% due to rounding.

Vendors

Table 36
Does your organization have formal guidelines for evaluating and selecting vendors?

		Organization Type		Number of FTEs					
	Total	Trade	IMO	2 or less	3-5	6-10	11-29	30-99	100 +
Number of Respondents	746	331	410	99	161	134	186	122	44
Yes	29%	22%	33%	15%	22%	24%	29%	43%	57%
No	71%	78%	67%	85%	78%	76%	71%	57%	43%

Table 37a
Does your organization use a process that requires multiple vendor bids when purchasing supplies and services?

		Organization Type		Number of FTEs					
	Total	Trade	IMO	2 or less	3-5	6-10	11-29	30-99	100 +
Number of Respondents	749	334	410	100	161	133	189	123	43
Yes	46%	39%	51%	30%	36%	47%	50%	56%	70%
No	54%	61%	49%	70%	64%	53%	50%	44%	30%

Table 37b
If yes, are multiple bids required for all purchases or only for those above a specified amount?

		Organization Type		Number of FTEs					
	Total	Trade	IMO	2 or less	3-5	6-10	11-29	30-99	100 +
Number of Respondents	320	121	196	28	54	60	83	66	29
All purchases require multiple bids	19%	13%	23%	21%	28%	15%	24%	12%	10%
Only purchases over a specified amount require multiple bids	81%	87%	77%	79%	72%	85%	76%	88%	90%

Table 37c
If yes, what amount?

		Organization Type		Number of FTEs					
	Total	Trade	IMO	2 or less	3-5	6-10	11-29	30-99	100 +
Number of Respondents	223	90	130	19	33	47	52	51	21
Mean	$8,139	$8,116	$8,220	$5,263	$7,356	$4,947	$5,687	$11,078	$18,052
Median	$5,000	$5,000	$5,000	$2,000	$5,000	$5,000	$5,000	$5,000	$10,000
25th Percentile	$1,000	$1,000	$1,000	$1,000	$1,000	$1,000	$1,000	$2,000	$4,250
75th Percentile	$10,000	$10,000	$7,500	$5,000	$6,250	$5,000	$10,000	$10,000	$25,000

⊕ Percentages add to more than 100% due to multiple responses.
*Too few responses to obtain statistically valid information.
**Mean can be distorted due to very extreme values.
Note: Percentages may add to more or less than 100% due to rounding.

Table 38
Who has the authority to make the final decision with regard to selecting vendors? ♦

	Total	Organization Type		Number of FTEs					
		Trade	IMO	2 or less	3-5	6-10	11-29	30-99	100 +
Number of Respondents	761	338	418	103	164	134	190	126	44
Chief staff executive	86%	87%	86%	83%	90%	94%	90%	75%	68%
Controller/CFO	26%	26%	26%	0%	5%	19%	38%	54%	57%
Department Head	30%	28%	31%	1%	5%	20%	42%	62%	75%
Deputy staff executive	11%	9%	12%	2%	2%	10%	15%	19%	23%
Finance or other committee	9%	6%	10%	11%	5%	12%	8%	10%	9%
Board of Directors	25%	23%	28%	45%	28%	31%	18%	14%	20%
Other	5%	6%	4%	5%	5%	4%	3%	8%	5%

♦ Percentages add to more than 100% due to multiple responses.
*Too few responses to obtain statistically valid information.
**Mean can be distorted due to very extreme values.
Note: Percentages may add to more or less than 100% due to rounding.

OFFICE MANAGEMENT

Summary of Major Findings

Staffing: A majority of all organizations, 59 percent, report having at least one full time equivalent (FTE) responsible for office management.

Responsibilities: People in this position are most likely to have the following responsibilities:

- Mail center (79 percent report that this is a responsibility of office management staff)
- Copy center/printing (72 percent)
- Reception (70 percent)
- Facilities maintenance and planning (69 percent)
- Inventory management (68 percent)
- Purchasing management (66 percent)

Office/Physical Plant: Leased space is the most frequently reported ownership status until 100+ FTEs is reached. The largest organizations are about equally likely to own a building and occupy part of it (31 percent), own and occupy an entire building (29 percent), or lease space in a building (29 percent). The median square feet occupied in the headquarters location is 5,000. Naturally the number of square feet occupied increases with the number of FTEs. Most expect no change in the next three years. There was no change in either ownership status or expectations of change between 2001 and this latest report.

Equipment Leasing: Most organizations lease copiers (64 percent), few lease computers (7 percent), or lease office furniture (2 percent).

Insurance: There have been increases in the percentage of organizations reporting carrying convention cancellation insurance between the P & P studies conducted in 2001 and 2005 from 29 percent to 37 percent. The incidence of umbrella and excess liability coverage has also increased from 56 to 63 percent. Other insurance coverage has remained constant between the two survey years.

Office Procedures: Most organizations report that routine mailings are handled in-house (88 percent) but many also report outsourcing mailings (54 percent). Clearly some organizations use a combination of methods. Use of bar coding has remained constant since 2001 with 30 percent of all organizations using bar codes.

The use of centralized purchasing for supplies and services has increased from 57 percent of all organizations in 2001 to 67 percent in 2005.

Disaster Preparedness: Questions about disaster plans are new to this study. In this era of heightened awareness it is surprising to find that disaster plans are not found in the majority of organizations. The existence of disaster plans is clearly correlated to the number of FTEs.

Perhaps this dearth of planning is due to the small number of organizations that reported having handled a disaster or media crisis in the past three years (21 percent).

Healthcare Organizations

All questions in the P & P were cross-tabulated by whether or not the responding organization's primary interest/subject area is in healthcare. The following tables show the statistically significant differences between healthcare and all other types of organization on data covered in this volume. If not shown below, responses received from healthcare organizations were similar to responses received by all other types of organization.

Does Organization Use Bar Coding in Mailings?			
		Organization Type	
Volume 3 Table 61	Total	Healthcare	All Other
Number of Respondents	667	108	559
Yes	30%	37%	29%
No	70%	63%	71%

Does Organization Have a Published Disaster Preparedness Plan?			
		Organization Type	
Volume 3 Table 64	Total	Healthcare	All Other
Number of Respondents	663	107	556
Yes	34%	40%	34%
No	66%	60%	66%

Does Organization's Human Resource System Have a Business Continuity Plan?			
		Organization Type	
Volume 3 Table 65a	Total	Healthcare	All Other
Number of Respondents	686	110	576
Yes	16%	21%	16%
No	84%	79%	84%

If yes, Has Organization's Business Continuity Plan Been Reviewed to Ensure HIPAA Regulations Are Met?			
		Organization Type	
Volume 3 Table 65b	Total	Healthcare	All Other
Number of Respondents	107	22	85
Yes	59%	73%	57%
No	41%	27%	43%

Index to Tables

Office Management

Table Number

Staffing:

Responsibilities

Office/Physical Plant

Equipment Leasing

Insurance

Office Procedures

Disaster Preparedness

Staffing

Table 39
Percent of organizations reporting at least 1 FTE in Office Management:

		Organization Type		Number of FTEs					
	Total	Trade	IMO	2 or less	3-5	6-10	11-29	30-99	100 +
Number of Respondents	1,004	459	539	142	180	168	246	192	76
At least 1 FTE in Office Management	59%	60%	57%	16%	49%	58%	72%	77%	75%

Responsibilities

Table 40
Areas of responsibility that apply to office management staff:⌖

		Organization Type		Number of FTEs					
	Total	Trade	IMO	2 or less	3-5	6-10	11-29	30-99	100 +
Number of Respondents	441	201	237	19	77	77	130	105	33
Copy center/print on demand center/reprographics	72%	73%	71%	63%	75%	66%	71%	75%	73%
Disaster preparedness/disaster recovery	44%	41%	46%	26%	26%	34%	46%	58%	61%
Facilities maintenance and planning	69%	69%	69%	32%	44%	60%	75%	90%	85%
Human resources	51%	50%	51%	37%	44%	58%	61%	47%	36%
Inventory management	68%	68%	68%	58%	70%	78%	70%	62%	61%
Mail center	79%	82%	77%	79%	73%	75%	78%	87%	85%
OSHA, workers' compensation and other regulatory areas	37%	36%	38%	32%	23%	36%	43%	41%	33%
Purchasing management	66%	68%	64%	58%	71%	68%	63%	65%	70%
Reception	70%	69%	71%	79%	69%	78%	73%	64%	61%
Risk insurance	37%	37%	38%	26%	31%	31%	42%	45%	33%
Security	49%	45%	52%	26%	29%	32%	52%	69%	70%
Other	5%	4%	5%	0%	0%	4%	5%	9%	6%

⌖ Percentages add to more than 100% due to multiple responses.
*Too few responses to obtain statistically valid information.
**Mean can be distorted due to very extreme values.
Note: Percentages may add to more or less than 100% due to rounding.

Office/Physical Plant

Table 41
Which of the following best describes the ownership status of your organization's headquarters?

		Organization Type		Number of FTEs					
	Total	Trade	IMO	2 or less	3-5	6-10	11-29	30-99	100 +
Number of Respondents	664	299	362	84	126	112	173	127	42
Owns a building in full or in part and occupies the entire building	21%	18%	23%	5%	17%	19%	25%	28%	29%
Owns a building in full or in part and occupies part of the entire building	12%	11%	13%	4%	6%	7%	17%	16%	31%
Leases an entire building	3%	3%	2%	0%	1%	4%	3%	4%	2%
Leases space in a building	56%	61%	52%	60%	70%	65%	50%	48%	29%
Headquarters is housed in multiple owned locations	1%	0%	1%	0%	0%	0%	1%	1%	5%
Headquarters is housed in multiple leased locations	1%	1%	1%	1%	0%	0%	1%	2%	2%
Headquarters is housed in multiple locations both leased and owned	<1%	0%	<1%	0%	0%	0%	0%	0%	2%
Other	7%	6%	7%	31%	6%	4%	3%	2%	0%

Table 42
What is the total square feet of space occupied by your organization's headquarters?

		Organization Type		Number of FTEs					
	Total	Trade	IMO	2 or less	3-5	6-10	11-29	30-99	100 +
Number of Respondents	606	270	333	70	119	108	160	113	36
Mean**	11,807	8,862	14,272	1,484	3,107	4,612	9,205	21,484	63,421
Median	5,000	4,500	5,500	875	1,850	3,650	7,000	18,755	51,000
25th percentile	2,000	2,000	2,000	500	1,000	2,600	5,000	12,615	34,077
75th percentile	12,000	10,500	15,000	1,500	2,800	5,090	10,500	27,768	77,250

Table 43
Is your organization planning to increase or decrease your office space in the next three years?

		Organization Type		Number of FTEs					
	Total	Trade	IMO	2 or less	3-5	6-10	11-29	30-99	100 +
Number of Respondents	669	301	365	86	126	114	173	128	42
Increase	24%	26%	23%	13%	20%	30%	28%	22%	33%
Decrease	6%	8%	5%	3%	10%	6%	3%	7%	12%
No change	70%	66%	72%	84%	70%	64%	69%	71%	55%

"ILTA's offices are 3500 sq. feet.

⧫ Percentages add to more than 100% due to multiple responses.
*Too few responses to obtain statistically valid information.
**Mean can be distorted due to very extreme values.
Note: Percentages may add to more or less than 100% due to rounding.

Equipment Leasing

Table 44

Does your organization lease the following items?[ǂ]

		Organization Type		Number of FTEs					
	Total	**Trade**	**IMO**	**2 or less**	**3-5**	**6-10**	**11-29**	**30-99**	**100 +**
Number of Respondents	671	302	366	87	127	114	173	128	42
Computers	7%	8%	7%	5%	4%	13%	8%	5%	14%
Copiers	64%	67%	62%	31%	54%	76%	72%	73%	67%
Office furniture	2%	1%	2%	5%	2%	4%	2%	0%	0%
Other equipment	29%	25%	32%	22%	26%	36%	29%	29%	29%

Insurance

Table 45

Does your organization currently carry any of the following casualty/risk insurance as a separate policy?[ǂ]

		Organization Type		Number of FTEs					
	Total	**Trade**	**IMO**	**2 or less**	**3-5**	**6-10**	**11-29**	**30-99**	**100 +**
Number of Respondents	671	302	366	87	127	114	173	128	42
Automobile liability	38%	45%	33%	18%	26%	28%	47%	52%	71%
General liability	84%	87%	81%	75%	91%	83%	86%	82%	83%
Convention cancellation	37%	31%	42%	18%	24%	33%	45%	48%	57%
Umbrella and excess liability	63%	65%	60%	29%	57%	65%	72%	73%	71%
Fire and related perils	52%	52%	51%	34%	42%	61%	52%	64%	52%
Other	17%	17%	18%	14%	14%	18%	18%	19%	24%

ǂ Percentages add to more than 100% due to multiple responses.
*Too few responses to obtain statistically valid information.
**Mean can be distorted due to very extreme values.
Note: Percentages may add to more or less than 100% due to rounding.

Office Procedures

Table 46
How are routine mailings handled?⁺

	Total	Organization Type		Number of FTEs					
		Trade	IMO	2 or less	3-5	6-10	11-29	30-99	100 +
Number of Respondents	671	302	366	87	127	114	173	128	42
In-house staff	88%	91%	86%	80%	87%	90%	90%	87%	90%
Outsourced	54%	45%	61%	44%	50%	59%	53%	55%	69%
In-house staff has converted routine mailings to e-mail, CD-ROM or another media	26%	24%	27%	9%	20%	26%	32%	30%	36%
Outsourced staff has converted routine mailings to e-mail, CD-ROM or another media	3%	2%	4%	2%	1%	2%	3%	4%	12%
Other	2%	2%	2%	5%	4%	0%	2%	1%	0%

Table 47
Does your organization routinely use bar coding in its mailings?

	Total	Organization Type		Number of FTEs					
		Trade	IMO	2 or less	3-5	6-10	11-29	30-99	100 +
Number of Respondents	667	300	364	87	126	113	173	127	41
Yes	30%	23%	36%	29%	25%	18%	31%	41%	49%
No	70%	77%	64%	71%	75%	82%	69%	59%	51%

Table 48
Does your organization have a centralized purchasing function for organizational supplies and services?

	Total	Organization Type		Number of FTEs					
		Trade	IMO	2 or less	3-5	6-10	11-29	30-99	100 +
Number of Respondents	667	300	364	87	125	114	173	127	41
Yes	67%	66%	67%	44%	58%	69%	71%	82%	71%
No	33%	34%	33%	56%	42%	31%	29%	18%	29%

⁺ Percentages add to more than 100% due to multiple responses.
*Too few responses to obtain statistically valid information.
**Mean can be distorted due to very extreme values.
Note: Percentages may add to more or less than 100% due to rounding.

Disaster Preparedness

Table 49
Has your organization handled a disaster/media crisis in the past 3 years?

		Organization Type		Number of FTEs					
	Total	Trade	IMO	2 or less	3-5	6-10	11-29	30-99	100 +
Number of Respondents	452	188	261	48	75	69	124	97	39
Yes	21%	24%	18%	8%	12%	16%	23%	26%	38%
No	79%	76%	82%	92%	88%	84%	77%	74%	62%

Table 50
Does your organization have a published disaster preparedness/recovery plan?

		Organization Type		Number of FTEs					
	Total	Trade	IMO	2 or less	3-5	6-10	11-29	30-99	100 +
Number of Respondents	663	297	363	86	126	112	172	126	41
Yes	34%	32%	37%	12%	18%	31%	38%	54%	63%
No	66%	68%	63%	88%	82%	69%	62%	46%	37%

Table 51a
Does your organization's human resource system have a business continuity plan?

		Organization Type		Number of FTEs					
	Total	Trade	IMO	2 or less	3-5	6-10	11-29	30-99	100 +
Number of Respondents	686	313	370	76	135	125	181	130	39
Yes	16%	15%	18%	8%	8%	9%	15%	28%	51%
No	84%	85%	82%	92%	92%	91%	85%	72%	49%

Table 51b
If yes, has your organization's business continuity plan been reviewed to ensure they meet HIPAA privacy and security regulations?

		Organization Type		Number of FTEs					
	Total	Trade	IMO	2 or less	3-5	6-10	11-29	30-99	100 +
Number of Respondents	107	46	60	6	10	11	25	36	19
Yes	59%	59%	58%	50%	60%	36%	60%	58%	74%
No	41%	41%	42%	50%	40%	64%	40%	42%	26%

⌖ Percentages add to more than 100% due to multiple responses.
*Too few responses to obtain statistically valid information.
**Mean can be distorted due to very extreme values.
Note: Percentages may add to more or less than 100% due to rounding.

Table 52
Does your organization's financial system have a business continuity plan?

	Total	Organization Type		Number of FTEs					
		Trade	IMO	2 or less	3-5	6-10	11-29	30-99	100 +
Number of Respondents	727	322	401	99	158	126	180	121	43
Yes	36%	36%	35%	16%	23%	31%	37%	55%	79%
No	64%	64%	65%	84%	77%	69%	63%	45%	21%

Table 53
Does your organization have a crisis plan to deal with such events as disasters, emergency communications or the media?

	Total	Organization Type		Number of FTEs					
		Trade	IMO	2 or less	3-5	6-10	11-29	30-99	100 +
Number of Respondents	453	189	261	47	79	69	124	98	36
Yes	44%	40%	47%	19%	28%	28%	44%	65%	83%
No	56%	60%	53%	81%	72%	72%	56%	35%	17%

ᵠ Percentages add to more than 100% due to multiple responses.
*Too few responses to obtain statistically valid information.
**Mean can be distorted due to very extreme values.
Note: Percentages may add to more or less than 100% due to rounding.